Li River In
Guilin

FACES
AND
PLACES

CHINA

BY PATRICK RYAN

THE CHILD'S WORLD®

Country
Facts

Area: 3,705,000 square miles.
That is a little larger than the United States.

Population: Over 1 billion people

Capital City: Beijing

Other Important Cities: Shanghai, Tianjin, Guangzhou

Money: The yuan. One yuan is divided into 10 jiao.

National Sport: Ping pong

National Holiday: National Day—October 1

Important Holiday: Chinese New Year. This holiday happens in late January or early February.

National Flag: A red flag with five yellow stars.
The four smaller stars represent the people of China. The big star represents China's government. The red color represents the revolution that created China.

Highest Mountain: Mount Everest. It is 29, 028 feet high. Mt. Everest is the highest mountain in the world.

Text copyright © 1998 by The Child's World®, Inc.
All rights reserved. No part of this book may be reproduced or utilized in any form or by any means without written permission from the publisher.
Printed in the United States of America.

Library of Congress Cataloging-in-Publication Data
Ryan, Pat (Patrick M.).
China / by Pat Ryan.
Series: "Faces and Places".
p. cm.
Includes index.
Summary: Describes the five major regions of China and briefly tells how people live there.
ISBN 1-56766-276-5

1. China — Juvenile literature. [1. China.] I. Title.
DS706.R93 1998
951 — dc20
96-13903
CIP
AC

GRAPHIC DESIGN
Robert A. Honey, Seattle

PHOTO RESEARCH
James R. Rothaus / James R. Rothaus & Associates

ELECTRONIC PRE–PRESS PRODUCTION
Robert E. Bonaker / Graphic Design & Consulting Co.

PHOTOGRAPHY
All photography from Dennis Cox / ChinaStock except for photo of Pu Yi on page 14 which was supplied by The National Archives / Corbis

Table
of
Contents

CHAPTER	PAGE

If you could float high above Earth, you would see huge land areas surrounded by water. These land areas are called continents. Most of the continents are made up of several countries. China is a huge country on the continent of Asia. China lies next to the Pacific Ocean.

Western Hemisphere

Eastern Hemisphere

China (white) is in the east and U.S.A. (green) is in the west

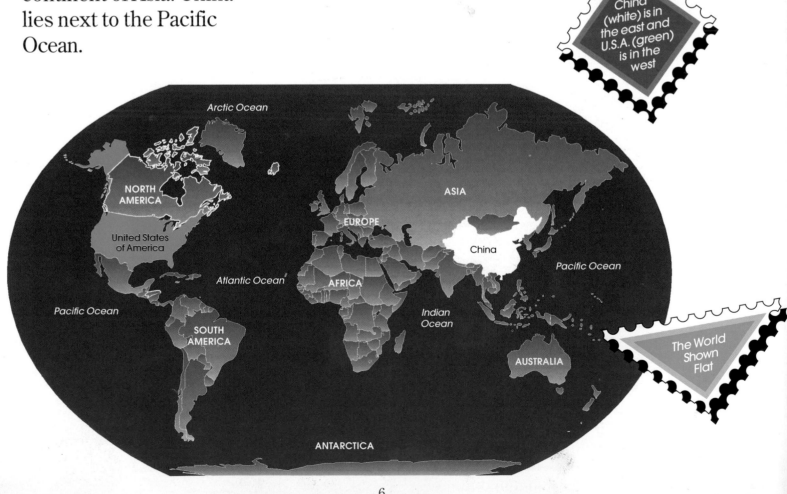

Arctic Ocean

NORTH AMERICA

ASIA

EUROPE

United States of America

China

Atlantic Ocean

AFRICA

Pacific Ocean

Pacific Ocean

Indian Ocean

SOUTH AMERICA

AUSTRALIA

The World Shown Flat

ANTARCTICA

RUSSIA

MONGOLIA

NORTH KOREA

SOUTH KOREA

JAPAN

CHINA

Himalaya Mountains

NEPAL

BHUTAN

BANGLADESH

INDIA

MYANMAR

TAIWAN

*Pacific
Ocean*

LAOS

VIETNAM

THAILAND

PHILIPPINES

*Indian
Ocean*

CAMBODIA

TIBETAN
PLATEAU

INNER MONGOLIA

Rice
Paddies

• Yangshuo

Green River
Near
Yangshuo

Since China is so big, there are many different land areas. Some areas are called *plateaus*. A plateau is a flat area that is higher than the other areas of land around it. The Inner Mongolian Plateau is an area in China that has bitterly cold winters, and very hot summers. The Tibetan Plateau is surrounded by rough, jagged mountains.

Inner Mongolian Plateau

Besides the plateaus, there are three other areas in China. The North China Plain is a flatter area that is surrounded by mountains on three sides. Central China has lots of people and huge cities. Southern China is covered with rice fields.

Rice Paddies In Southern China

Spring Thaw On Tibetan Plateau

China has many different kinds of plants and animals. In fact, it is home to some of the world's most interesting creatures. One of the best known animals in China is the panda. It lives in the bamboo forests of China and Tibet. Pandas eat bamboo plants that grow in the forests.

Yaks are wild cows that live in the snowy mountain areas of China. They have long, shaggy hair that covers their body. This hair keeps them warm and dry. The yaks travel high in the mountains on dangerous paths. From far away, the big yaks look like boats on a white sea! That's why many people call them "ships of the plateau."

Panda Nibbles On Bamboo Leaves

Tibetan Yak

Tibetan
Yak

Pandas

● Guangxi

Water Buffalo
of Guangxi

The Great Wall
of China

Great Wall
of China

Beijing

Xi'an

China is a very old country. Until recently, China was ruled by kings, called *emperors*. Emperors were born into families of rulers. These royal families were called dynasties. China may have been named for the Qin (ch'in) *dynasty*.

Terra Cotta Army in Xi'an

The first emperor, Qin Shihuangdi, belonged to the Qin dynasty. Long ago, Shihuangdi built a wall across northern China to keep out his enemies. This wall was almost 6,000 miles long! Today we call it the Great Wall. Almost half of it is still standing.

Imperial Palace In Beijing

China's last emperor was a six-year-old boy named Pu Yi. Many people disagreed with the way Pu Yi was ruling the country. In 1912, he and his government were overthrown by Dr. Sun Yat-sen and the Nationalist Republican Army. When people overthrow their rulers, it is called a revolution.

In 1949, a new government formed under a man named Mao Zedong (MA-oh SAY-dong) This government believed in an idea called *communism.* Governments that practice communism believe that property should belong to the whole country instead of individual people. China is one of the few countries that still practices communism today.

Dr. Sun Yat-sen

Pu Yi The Last Emperor

Young Girls With Chinese Flags

Beijing •

Portrait of
Mao Zedong
In Beijing

Crowded Street In Shanghai

Beijing •
Hebei •
• Shanghai
• Nanjing

The People

China has the most people of any country in the world—over one billion. If all the people in China held hands, they would circle the world 38 times! With so many people, the biggest problem in China is making sure that everyone has enough to eat. All of China's people need food, but there just isn't enough for everyone! To keep the population from growing too much, the government has said that families should have only one child.

One-Child Family From Hebei

Pedestrians On Nanjing Road

Police From Beijing

Bicyclists
In
Beijing

Over 200 million people live in China's cities. Some city people live in large apartment buildings. Others live in small houses with tile roofs. China's cities are so crowded, people don't use cars. Instead, they move from place to place on bicycles! Many people also travel on trains.

Country life in China is very different from city life. Many country people live in houses with only two rooms—a kitchen and a bathroom. Most of them work as farmers. Other families live on small cargo boats called *sampans*. People who live on sampans carry goods up and down the rivers. In the mountain areas of China, some country people live in caves.

Hulun
Buyr
Grassland
Farm

Hulun Buyr

Beijing

Grand Canal

Living On The
Grand
Canal

Wuhan

Shanghai

Chinese children start school when they are seven years old. They begin each day at 8:30 in the morning—with ten minutes of exercise! In school, Chinese students learn to write when they are very young. They also learn how to do math by moving beads on an *abacus*. An abacus is a very old tool for counting. After some classes, Chinese students take a two-hour lunch. The school day ends at 4:30.

Morning
Excercises
In Wuhan

Almost everyone in China speaks Chinese, but they don't all speak it the same way. That means that a Chinese speaker from one area might not be able to understand Chinese in another area. China's official language is Mandarin Chinese, which is spoken in the north. People in the south speak many different kinds of Chinese, including Cantonese.

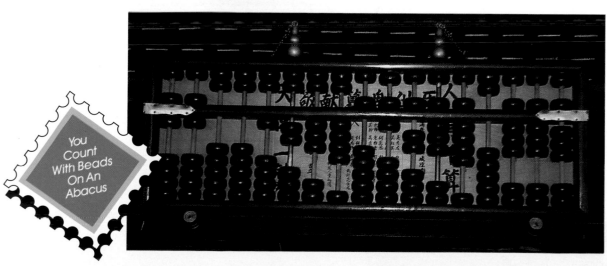

You
Count
With Beads
On An
Abacus

Work

Yantai Fisherman

More than half of all Chinese people are farmers. They grow rice, wheat, grains, and other crops like cotton and tea. They also raise pigs and chickens. Many Chinese farmers still do all their work by hand, or with a plow pulled by an animal.

Shoe Factory Worker

Beijing Pottery Painter

China is growing and changing every day. Today, millions of people work in factories instead of farming. They make televisions, radios, and video games.

They also make clothes, shoes, sports equipment, and toys. The things China makes are sold all over the world.

Beijing •
• Yantai

Hainan Island

Pepper
Workers
On Hainan
Island

Chengdu Street
Market

Beijing
• Chengdu

Anhui
Province

Food

The Chinese food that you eat is probably not the same as the food in China. A real Chinese snack would be shark fins, seaweed, slugs, frogs, jellyfish, pigs ears, chicken feet, or even birds-nest soup! These are all favorite foods in China. Chinese people also like to eat beef, chicken, and vegetables, just like you.

The Chinese serve many foods with rice or noodles. And instead of using forks, people eat with special sticks called *chopsticks*. Chopsticks are used by either scooping or pinching food to lift it up to a person's mouth. Chinese people also have their favorite drink with most meals—tea! China grows some of the best tea in the world.

An Anhui Province Boy With Chopsticks

Family-Style Eating In Beijing

Beijing Opera

People in China enjoy music, plays, movies and sports. Ping pong, swimming, volleyball, gymnastics, and soccer are all favorite sports. Another favorite table game is called mah-jongg. It is similar to the card game called rummy. But it is played with small tiles instead of cards.

Every morning, millions of people exercise by performing *t'ai chi chuan* (TIE chi CHON) in parks and courtyards. Tai chi is an ancient form of exercise that has 128 different movements. The movements are slow and graceful. Many people also like to do forms of self-defense called *martial arts*. There are many forms of martial arts, including karate and judo.

Outdoor Ping Pong In Beijing

Beijing •

Hangzhou •

Morning
Excercises
In Hangzhou

Spring Festival
In Beijing

Beijing •

Guilin •

Dragon
Dance
In
Beijing

The Chinese people love holidays. The biggest celebration in China is the Spring Festival. Another name for this holiday is the Chinese New Year. It is celebrated in January or February. The actual date of the Chinese New Year depends on where the moon is in the sky. This date changes every year.

Guilin
Cormorant
Fisherman

China is an interesting place. It is home to many different kinds of plants and animals. There are hundreds of old buildings to visit. And China has some of the most beautiful countrysides in the world. The Chinese people are polite to strangers and they welcome visitors from other countries. So if you ever go to China, be sure to smile—China will smile back!

China is really called "The People's Republic of China."
People just say "China" for short.

Tho Groat Wall of China is the only man-made object that
can be seen from outer space.

Birds are the only pets city people can own. Many older
Chinese men like to take their pet birds to the park. There
they teach their songbirds to sing.

China is a very old country. Three thousand years ago,
Chinese people were already living in towns. They had even
invented a way to write!

	CHINESE	HOW TO SAY IT
Hello	ni hao	(nee-how)
Goodbye	zai jian	(tziy jehn)
Please	qing	(ching)
Thank You	xiexie	(shyeh shyeh)
One	yi	(ee)
Two	er	(ahr)
Three	san	(sahn)
China	Zhongguo	(jawng-gwaw)

Glossary

abacus (AB–uh–kuss)
An abacus is a very old tool that is used for counting. It works by sliding beads along a groove.

communism (COM–yuh–ni–zum)
Communism is an idea that some governments use to rule their countries. Governments that practice communism believe that property should belong to the whole country instead of individual people.

continent (KON–tuh–nent)
All of the land areas on Earth are divided up into huge sections called continents. Most of the continents are separated by oceans.

chopsticks (CHOP–stiks)
Chopsticks are special sticks that people in China use to eat with. Chopsticks are used by either scooping or pinching food to lift it up to a person's mouth.

dynasty (DY–nuh–stee)
A dynasty is a family of rulers. Each one of China's emperors came from a dynasty.

emperor (EM–pur–ur)
An emperor is what the king of China is called. Today, China's emperors do not rule the country.

lion dance (LIE–un DANS)
In a lion dance, several people dress up like a lion. Then they dance around. People light firecrackers and play loud music during lion dances.

martial arts (MAR–shul ARTS)
Martial arts are forms of self-defense. There are many forms of martial arts, including karate and judo.

plateau (pla–TOH)
A plateau is a flat area that is higher than the other areas of land around it. Some areas of China are plateaus.

revolution (re-vuh–LOO–shun)
When people overthrow their rulers, it is called a revolution.

sampans (SAM–panz)
Sampans are small cargo boats. They are used to carry goods up and down rivers.

Index